PRACTICE JOURNAL

Juanita Robinson

BrainSwell Publishing
Ingersoll, Ontario

Copyright © 2019 Juanita Robinson

All rights reserved. The use of any part of this publication reproduced, transmitted in any form or by any means, electronic, mechanical, photocopying, recording, or otherwise, or stored in a retrieval system, without the prior written consent of the publisher is an infringement of the copyright law.

ISBN 978-1-989296-08-0

Cover Design copyright © Juanita Robinson

BrainSwell Publishing
Ingersoll, ON

Welcome Singers!

I want you to become the singer you've always wanted to be, which is why I created this practice resource. By recording what you practice, when you practice it, how it feels, and more, you'll start to see patterns. When it's on paper, you might realize that practicing five days a week is better for your vocal recovery than practicing six. Or, you might see that when you skip your warm-ups, your range suffers, and your tone quality just sounds dull.

You don't need to fill in every blank or feel guilty when you miss a day, or two... or six.
Singing is a skill, but it's also a way to express your joys, triumphs, frustrations, and sorrows. This resource is here to open your eyes to understanding yourself as a vocalist and aid in equipping you to achieve your goals.

How to use this Vocal Journal

Please bring this journal to your lessons so that as your teacher gives you vocal exercises, you can write them down under the appropriate heading (breath support, head voice, mix, etc.). Then when you're practicing at home, you can look back at the exercises and choose what you want to work on.

It's important to set out goals. Once you have a goal, all you need is a guide and a map, and you'll be well on your way. Your voice teacher is your guide, and you and your teacher should be in constant communication about your map. This vocal journal is where you'll keep all your tools for your map. For example, when you're wanting to work on extending your vocal range up, you might want to spend some extra time working on your flageolet exercises. Or, if you're feeling like you keep running out of air prematurely, check out what you've recorded in your breath support exercise section.

There are so many wonderful teachers out there, and with the internet, location never needs to prevent you from accessing high-quality vocal training! I love hearing from vocalists, and so if you've picked up this vocal journal and are using it, I would love to hear from you. Or, if you have any questions about this vocal journal or suggestions, I would appreciate you taking the time to send me a message and share your thoughts. You can always contact me through my website at www.jrvocals.com

Finally, I cannot let you begin without some inspiration:

"To play a wrong note is insignificant; to play without passion is inexcusable."
--Ludwig van Beethoven

"Take chances, make mistakes, and get messy."
--Miss. Frizzle

"Loud and proud; strong and wrong."
--Me... okay, maybe focus on the other two

Enjoy!

Using your Go-to Guides

Preparing your voice to sing is much like preparing your body to play sports—you need to warm up the muscles, stretch, and then train each muscle to act and react the way you want it to.
There are so many muscles you use when you sing. Different muscles are used when you're singing in different registers, so it makes sense to use specific exercises that will isolate those muscles and train them to act and respond the way you want them to.

You'll notice that your practice log only has 6 days to fill in. This is because you need at least one day of rest. Rest is important!

Three equal parts to your practice time

<u>1 Part Warm-ups</u>
You want to warm up your instrument. Spend 1/3 of your practice time working in your various registers to warm them up and get them ready and flexible to work. The basic registers you'll want to work on are Flageolet, Head, Falsetto, Chest, and Mix.

<u>1 Part Technique Training</u>
This is where you decide on your focus for your practice time. What are you wanting to refine or build? Do you have a bad habit that you need to stop? Is there a vocal goal that you have that you want to invest some time working on? Some possible concepts that you might choose to focus on are:

- Vocal flexibility
- Extending your range
- Pitch
- Vibrato
- Riffs
- Breath Support
- Transitioning through your passagio/bridge
  and more...

<u>1 Part Song Work</u>
Now's your chance to apply all of your hard work to your song. Singing the song from beginning to end, however, doesn't really benefit you if that's all you do. Sing the song through and then when you get to a problem spot, stop! That's where you focus. Figure out what's going wrong and apply your technique training to that area.

Remember...
Some days you won't have 30-60 minutes to do all this work. That's okay... life happens. On those days, try to just spend time working through warm-ups in your different registers as well as light technique work—this can be done in the car or as you're getting ready for your day. This doesn't have to be an "all or nothing" experience.

Vocal Technique Go-to Guide Example

Exercise	Pattern	Register	Purpose
gohng-ong-ong	*5-4-3-2-1*	*mix*	*Use the strength from chest voice and flexibility of nasals to help navigate through transition point*
mah-on-non	*1__5-3-1*	*mix*	*The m gives nasal resonance and the ah is chesty (strong) and then going up into transition point, the on is more flexible and heady*
non (French sounding)	*5-3-1*	*mix*	*The n gives nasal resonance which helps to add flexibility through the transition point where I might normally tense up*

Warm-up Go-to Guide

General Warm-ups

Exercise	Pattern
lip trills	1-3-5-8-5-3-1
mum	1-3-5-3-1

Breath Support

Exercise	Pattern
shoo (slow slide)	5_____1
mum	1-3-5-3-1-3-5-3-1-3-5-3-1

Flageolet → Stretch

Exercise	Pattern
kyoo	3-1
mw	5-3-1

Head & Falsetto

Exercise	Pattern
goo	5-5-5-3-1
whoop	8-5-3-1

Chest

Exercise	Pattern
hey!	5-4-3-2-1
gohg	5-3-1

Mix

Exercise	Pattern
meow	1-3-5-5-5-3-1
gwahm	5-3-1

Week: *July 14 – 20*

This week's focus: *Work on transition point. Make it smooth without tension.*

Notes from my voice lesson: *Watch out for neck and jaw tension when approaching transition point.*

Practice Log

	Day 1	Day 2	Day 3
Time of day	7:15am		
Before practice I feel…	Tired		
Concept I'm working on	Transition point/passagio		
Warm-ups	(Yes) / No	Yes / No	Yes / No
Technique exercises	gohng 5-4-3-2-1 mah-on-non 1_5-3-1 French non 5-3-1		
What went well or didn't go well with the technique exercises	mah-on-non went awesome! Was able to breeze through B4 without tension.		
Song name	Forever		
What went well	Chorus felt better than normal—less tense		
What needs Work	Bridge of the song feels and sounds too high if I jump the octave like in the recording		
After practice I feel…	Satisfied, happy		

Notes:

Practice Log

Repertoire

Songs I'd like to work on	Songs I've mastered	Key

Repertoire

Songs I'd like to work on	Songs I've mastered	Key

Repertoire

Songs I'd like to work on	Songs I've mastered	Key

Warm-up Go-to Guide

General Warm-ups

Exercise	Pattern

Breath Support

Exercise	Pattern

Warm-up Go-to Guide

Flageolet → Stretch

Exercise	Pattern

Head & Falsetto

Exercise	Pattern

Warm-up Go-to Guide

Chest

Exercise	Pattern

Mix

Exercise	Pattern

Vocal Technique Go-to Guide

Exercise	Pattern	Register	Purpose

Vocal Technique Go-to Guide

Exercise	Pattern	Register	Purpose

Vocal Technique Go-to Guide

Exercise	Pattern	Register	Purpose

Notes:

Week: _____

This week's focus:

Notes from my voice lesson:

Practice Log

	Day 1	Day 2	Day 3
Time of day			
Before practice I feel…			
Concept I'm working on			
Warm-ups	Yes / No	Yes / No	Yes / No
Technique exercises			
What went well or didn't go well with the technique exercises			
Song name			
What went well			
What needs Work			
After practice I feel…			

Time invested this week:

Day 1	Day 2	Day 3	Day 4	Day 5	Day 6
_____ min.	_____ min.	_____ min.	_____ min.	_____ min.	_____ min.

Problems I'm having or questions to ask at my next voice lesson:

Practice Log

	Day 4	Day 5	Day 6
Time of day			
Before practice I feel...			
Concept I'm working on			
Warm-ups	Yes / No	Yes / No	Yes / No
Technique exercises			
What went well or didn't go well with the technique exercises			
Song name			
What went well			
What needs work			
After practice I feel...			

Week: _____

This week's focus:

Notes from my voice lesson:

Practice Log

	Day 1	Day 2	Day 3
Time of day			
Before practice I feel...			
Concept I'm working on			
Warm-ups	Yes / No	Yes / No	Yes / No
Technique exercises			
What went well or didn't go well with the technique exercises			
Song name			
What went well			
What needs Work			
After practice I feel...			

Time invested this week:

Day 1	Day 2	Day 3	Day 4	Day 5	Day 6
_____ min.	_____ min.	_____ min.	_____ min.	_____ min.	_____ min.

Problems I'm having or questions to ask at my next voice lesson:

Practice Log

	Day 4	Day 5	Day 6
Time of day			
Before practice I feel...			
Concept I'm working on			
Warm-ups	Yes / No	Yes / No	Yes / No
Technique exercises			
What went well or didn't go well with the technique exercises			
Song name			
What went well			
What needs work			
After practice I feel...			

Week: _____

This week's focus:

Notes from my voice lesson:

Practice Log

	Day 1	Day 2	Day 3
Time of day			
Before practice I feel…			
Concept I'm working on			
Warm-ups	Yes / No	Yes / No	Yes / No
Technique exercises			
What went well or didn't go well with the technique exercises			
Song name			
What went well			
What needs Work			
After practice I feel…			

Time invested this week:

Day 1	Day 2	Day 3	Day 4	Day 5	Day 6
_____ min.	_____ min.	_____ min.	_____ min.	_____ min.	_____ min.

Problems I'm having or questions to ask at my next voice lesson:

Practice Log

	Day 4	Day 5	Day 6
Time of day			
Before practice I feel...			
Concept I'm working on			
Warm-ups	Yes / No	Yes / No	Yes / No
Technique exercises			
What went well or didn't go well with the technique exercises			
Song name			
What went well			
What needs work			
After practice I feel...			

Week: _____

This week's focus:

Notes from my voice lesson:

Practice Log

	Day 1	Day 2	Day 3
Time of day			
Before practice I feel…			
Concept I'm working on			
Warm-ups	Yes / No	Yes / No	Yes / No
Technique exercises			
What went well or didn't go well with the technique exercises			
Song name			
What went well			
What needs Work			
After practice I feel…			

Time invested this week:

Day 1	Day 2	Day 3	Day 4	Day 5	Day 6
_____ min.	_____ min.	_____ min.	_____ min.	_____ min.	_____ min.

Problems I'm having or questions to ask at my next voice lesson:

Practice Log

	Day 4	Day 5	Day 6
Time of day			
Before practice I feel...			
Concept I'm working on			
Warm-ups	Yes / No	Yes / No	Yes / No
Technique exercises			
What went well or didn't go well with the technique exercises			
Song name			
What went well			
What needs work			
After practice I feel...			

Week: _____

This week's focus:

Notes from my voice lesson:

Practice Log

	Day 1	Day 2	Day 3
Time of day			
Before practice I feel…			
Concept I'm working on			
Warm-ups	Yes / No	Yes / No	Yes / No
Technique exercises			
What went well or didn't go well with the technique exercises			
Song name			
What went well			
What needs Work			
After practice I feel…			

Time invested this week:

Day 1	Day 2	Day 3	Day 4	Day 5	Day 6
_____ min.	_____ min.	_____ min.	_____ min.	_____ min.	_____ min.

Problems I'm having or questions to ask at my next voice lesson:

Practice Log

	Day 4	Day 5	Day 6
Time of day			
Before practice I feel…			
Concept I'm working on			
Warm-ups	Yes / No	Yes / No	Yes / No
Technique exercises			
What went well or didn't go well with the technique exercises			
Song name			
What went well			
What needs work			
After practice I feel…			

Week: _____

This week's focus:

Notes from my voice lesson:

Practice Log

	Day 1	Day 2	Day 3
Time of day			
Before practice I feel...			
Concept I'm working on			
Warm-ups	Yes / No	Yes / No	Yes / No
Technique exercises			
What went well or didn't go well with the technique exercises			
Song name			
What went well			
What needs Work			
After practice I feel...			

Time invested this week:

Day 1	Day 2	Day 3	Day 4	Day 5	Day 6
_____ min.	_____ min.	_____ min.	_____ min.	_____ min.	_____ min.

Problems I'm having or questions to ask at my next voice lesson:

Practice Log

	Day 4	Day 5	Day 6
Time of day			
Before practice I feel...			
Concept I'm working on			
Warm-ups	Yes / No	Yes / No	Yes / No
Technique exercises			
What went well or didn't go well with the technique exercises			
Song name			
What went well			
What needs work			
After practice I feel...			

Week: _____

This week's focus:

Notes from my voice lesson:

Practice Log

	Day 1	Day 2	Day 3
Time of day			
Before practice I feel…			
Concept I'm working on			
Warm-ups	Yes / No	Yes / No	Yes / No
Technique exercises			
What went well or didn't go well with the technique exercises			
Song name			
What went well			
What needs Work			
After practice I feel…			

Time invested this week:

Day 1	Day 2	Day 3	Day 4	Day 5	Day 6
_____ min.	_____ min.	_____ min.	_____ min.	_____ min.	_____ min.

Problems I'm having or questions to ask at my next voice lesson:

Practice Log

	Day 4	Day 5	Day 6
Time of day			
Before practice I feel…			
Concept I'm working on			
Warm-ups	Yes / No	Yes / No	Yes / No
Technique exercises			
What went well or didn't go well with the technique exercises			
Song name			
What went well			
What needs work			
After practice I feel…			

Week: _____

This week's focus:

Notes from my voice lesson:

Practice Log

	Day 1	Day 2	Day 3
Time of day			
Before practice I feel…			
Concept I'm working on			
Warm-ups	Yes / No	Yes / No	Yes / No
Technique exercises			
What went well or didn't go well with the technique exercises			
Song name			
What went well			
What needs Work			
After practice I feel…			

Time invested this week:

Day 1	Day 2	Day 3	Day 4	Day 5	Day 6
_____ min.	_____ min.	_____ min.	_____ min.	_____ min.	_____ min.

Problems I'm having or questions to ask at my next voice lesson:

Practice Log

	Day 4	Day 5	Day 6
Time of day			
Before practice I feel…			
Concept I'm working on			
Warm-ups	Yes / No	Yes / No	Yes / No
Technique exercises			
What went well or didn't go well with the technique exercises			
Song name			
What went well			
What needs work			
After practice I feel…			

Week: _____

This week's focus:

Notes from my voice lesson:

Practice Log

	Day 1	Day 2	Day 3
Time of day			
Before practice I feel...			
Concept I'm working on			
Warm-ups	Yes / No	Yes / No	Yes / No
Technique exercises			
What went well or didn't go well with the technique exercises			
Song name			
What went well			
What needs Work			
After practice I feel...			

Time invested this week:

Day 1	Day 2	Day 3	Day 4	Day 5	Day 6
_____ min.	_____ min.	_____ min.	_____ min.	_____ min.	_____ min.

Problems I'm having or questions to ask at my next voice lesson:

Practice Log

	Day 4	Day 5	Day 6
Time of day			
Before practice I feel...			
Concept I'm working on			
Warm-ups	Yes / No	Yes / No	Yes / No
Technique exercises			
What went well or didn't go well with the technique exercises			
Song name			
What went well			
What needs work			
After practice I feel...			

Week: _____

This week's focus:

Notes from my voice lesson:

Practice Log

	Day 1	Day 2	Day 3
Time of day			
Before practice I feel…			
Concept I'm working on			
Warm-ups	Yes / No	Yes / No	Yes / No
Technique exercises			
What went well or didn't go well with the technique exercises			
Song name			
What went well			
What needs Work			
After practice I feel…			

Time invested this week:

Day 1	Day 2	Day 3	Day 4	Day 5	Day 6
_____ min.	_____ min.	_____ min.	_____ min.	_____ min.	_____ min.

Problems I'm having or questions to ask at my next voice lesson:

Practice Log

	Day 4	Day 5	Day 6
Time of day			
Before practice I feel...			
Concept I'm working on			
Warm-ups	Yes / No	Yes / No	Yes / No
Technique exercises			
What went well or didn't go well with the technique exercises			
Song name			
What went well			
What needs work			
After practice I feel...			

Week: _____

This week's focus:

Notes from my voice lesson:

Practice Log

	Day 1	Day 2	Day 3
Time of day			
Before practice I feel...			
Concept I'm working on			
Warm-ups	Yes / No	Yes / No	Yes / No
Technique exercises			
What went well or didn't go well with the technique exercises			
Song name			
What went well			
What needs Work			
After practice I feel...			

Time invested this week:

Day 1	Day 2	Day 3	Day 4	Day 5	Day 6
_____ min.	_____ min.	_____ min.	_____ min.	_____ min.	_____ min.

Problems I'm having or questions to ask at my next voice lesson:

Practice Log

	Day 4	Day 5	Day 6
Time of day			
Before practice I feel...			
Concept I'm working on			
Warm-ups	Yes / No	Yes / No	Yes / No
Technique exercises			
What went well or didn't go well with the technique exercises			
Song name			
What went well			
What needs work			
After practice I feel...			

Week: _____

This week's focus:

Notes from my voice lesson:

Practice Log

	Day 1	Day 2	Day 3
Time of day			
Before practice I feel...			
Concept I'm working on			
Warm-ups	Yes / No	Yes / No	Yes / No
Technique exercises			
What went well or didn't go well with the technique exercises			
Song name			
What went well			
What needs Work			
After practice I feel...			

Time invested this week:

Day 1	Day 2	Day 3	Day 4	Day 5	Day 6
_____ min.	_____ min.	_____ min.	_____ min.	_____ min.	_____ min.

Problems I'm having or questions to ask at my next voice lesson:

Practice Log

	Day 4	Day 5	Day 6
Time of day			
Before practice I feel...			
Concept I'm working on			
Warm-ups	Yes / No	Yes / No	Yes / No
Technique exercises			
What went well or didn't go well with the technique exercises			
Song name			
What went well			
What needs work			
After practice I feel...			

Week: _____

This week's focus:

Notes from my voice lesson:

Practice Log

	Day 1	Day 2	Day 3
Time of day			
Before practice I feel…			
Concept I'm working on			
Warm-ups	Yes / No	Yes / No	Yes / No
Technique exercises			
What went well or didn't go well with the technique exercises			
Song name			
What went well			
What needs Work			
After practice I feel…			

Time invested this week:

Day 1	Day 2	Day 3	Day 4	Day 5	Day 6
_____ min.	_____ min.	_____ min.	_____ min.	_____ min.	_____ min.

Problems I'm having or questions to ask at my next voice lesson:

Practice Log

	Day 4	Day 5	Day 6
Time of day			
Before practice I feel…			
Concept I'm working on			
Warm-ups	Yes / No	Yes / No	Yes / No
Technique exercises			
What went well or didn't go well with the technique exercises			
Song name			
What went well			
What needs work			
After practice I feel…			

Week: _____

This week's focus:

Notes from my voice lesson:

Practice Log

	Day 1	Day 2	Day 3
Time of day			
Before practice I feel…			
Concept I'm working on			
Warm-ups	Yes / No	Yes / No	Yes / No
Technique exercises			
What went well or didn't go well with the technique exercises			
Song name			
What went well			
What needs Work			
After practice I feel…			

Time invested this week:

Day 1	Day 2	Day 3	Day 4	Day 5	Day 6
_____ min.	_____ min.	_____ min.	_____ min.	_____ min.	_____ min.

Problems I'm having or questions to ask at my next voice lesson:

Practice Log

	Day 4	Day 5	Day 6
Time of day			
Before practice I feel...			
Concept I'm working on			
Warm-ups	Yes / No	Yes / No	Yes / No
Technique exercises			
What went well or didn't go well with the technique exercises			
Song name			
What went well			
What needs work			
After practice I feel...			

Week: _____

This week's focus:

Notes from my voice lesson:

Practice Log

	Day 1	Day 2	Day 3
Time of day			
Before practice I feel…			
Concept I'm working on			
Warm-ups	Yes / No	Yes / No	Yes / No
Technique exercises			
What went well or didn't go well with the technique exercises			
Song name			
What went well			
What needs Work			
After practice I feel…			

Time invested this week:

Day 1	Day 2	Day 3	Day 4	Day 5	Day 6
_____ min.	_____ min.	_____ min.	_____ min.	_____ min.	_____ min.

Problems I'm having or questions to ask at my next voice lesson:

Practice Log

	Day 4	Day 5	Day 6
Time of day			
Before practice I feel...			
Concept I'm working on			
Warm-ups	Yes / No	Yes / No	Yes / No
Technique exercises			
What went well or didn't go well with the technique exercises			
Song name			
What went well			
What needs work			
After practice I feel...			

Week: _____

This week's focus:

Notes from my voice lesson:

Practice Log

	Day 1	Day 2	Day 3
Time of day			
Before practice I feel…			
Concept I'm working on			
Warm-ups	Yes / No	Yes / No	Yes / No
Technique exercises			
What went well or didn't go well with the technique exercises			
Song name			
What went well			
What needs Work			
After practice I feel…			

Time invested this week:

Day 1	Day 2	Day 3	Day 4	Day 5	Day 6
_____ min.	_____ min.	_____ min.	_____ min.	_____ min.	_____ min.

Problems I'm having or questions to ask at my next voice lesson:

Practice Log

	Day 4	Day 5	Day 6
Time of day			
Before practice I feel…			
Concept I'm working on			
Warm-ups	Yes / No	Yes / No	Yes / No
Technique exercises			
What went well or didn't go well with the technique exercises			
Song name			
What went well			
What needs work			
After practice I feel…			

Week: _____

This week's focus:

Notes from my voice lesson:

Practice Log

	Day 1	Day 2	Day 3
Time of day			
Before practice I feel...			
Concept I'm working on			
Warm-ups	Yes / No	Yes / No	Yes / No
Technique exercises			
What went well or didn't go well with the technique exercises			
Song name			
What went well			
What needs Work			
After practice I feel...			

Time invested this week:

Day 1	Day 2	Day 3	Day 4	Day 5	Day 6
_____ min.	_____ min.	_____ min.	_____ min.	_____ min.	_____ min.

Problems I'm having or questions to ask at my next voice lesson:

Practice Log

	Day 4	Day 5	Day 6
Time of day			
Before practice I feel...			
Concept I'm working on			
Warm-ups	Yes / No	Yes / No	Yes / No
Technique exercises			
What went well or didn't go well with the technique exercises			
Song name			
What went well			
What needs work			
After practice I feel...			

Week: _____

This week's focus:

Notes from my voice lesson:

Practice Log

	Day 1	Day 2	Day 3
Time of day			
Before practice I feel…			
Concept I'm working on			
Warm-ups	Yes / No	Yes / No	Yes / No
Technique exercises			
What went well or didn't go well with the technique exercises			
Song name			
What went well			
What needs Work			
After practice I feel…			

Time invested this week:

Day 1	Day 2	Day 3	Day 4	Day 5	Day 6
_____ min.	_____ min.	_____ min.	_____ min.	_____ min.	_____ min.

Problems I'm having or questions to ask at my next voice lesson:

Practice Log

	Day 4	Day 5	Day 6
Time of day			
Before practice I feel...			
Concept I'm working on			
Warm-ups	Yes / No	Yes / No	Yes / No
Technique exercises			
What went well or didn't go well with the technique exercises			
Song name			
What went well			
What needs work			
After practice I feel...			

Week: _____

This week's focus:

Notes from my voice lesson:

Practice Log

	Day 1	Day 2	Day 3
Time of day			
Before practice I feel…			
Concept I'm working on			
Warm-ups	Yes / No	Yes / No	Yes / No
Technique exercises			
What went well or didn't go well with the technique exercises			
Song name			
What went well			
What needs Work			
After practice I feel…			

Time invested this week:

Day 1	Day 2	Day 3	Day 4	Day 5	Day 6
_____ min.	_____ min.	_____ min.	_____ min.	_____ min.	_____ min.

Problems I'm having or questions to ask at my next voice lesson:

Practice Log

	Day 4	Day 5	Day 6
Time of day			
Before practice I feel…			
Concept I'm working on			
Warm-ups	Yes / No	Yes / No	Yes / No
Technique exercises			
What went well or didn't go well with the technique exercises			
Song name			
What went well			
What needs work			
After practice I feel…			

Week: _____

This week's focus:

Notes from my voice lesson:

Practice Log

	Day 1	Day 2	Day 3
Time of day			
Before practice I feel…			
Concept I'm working on			
Warm-ups	Yes / No	Yes / No	Yes / No
Technique exercises			
What went well or didn't go well with the technique exercises			
Song name			
What went well			
What needs Work			
After practice I feel…			

Time invested this week:

Day 1	Day 2	Day 3	Day 4	Day 5	Day 6
_____ min.	_____ min.	_____ min.	_____ min.	_____ min.	_____ min.

Problems I'm having or questions to ask at my next voice lesson:

Practice Log

	Day 4	Day 5	Day 6
Time of day			
Before practice I feel...			
Concept I'm working on			
Warm-ups	Yes / No	Yes / No	Yes / No
Technique exercises			
What went well or didn't go well with the technique exercises			
Song name			
What went well			
What needs work			
After practice I feel...			

Week: _____

This week's focus:

Notes from my voice lesson:

Practice Log

	Day 1	Day 2	Day 3
Time of day			
Before practice I feel…			
Concept I'm working on			
Warm-ups	Yes / No	Yes / No	Yes / No
Technique exercises			
What went well or didn't go well with the technique exercises			
Song name			
What went well			
What needs Work			
After practice I feel…			

Time invested this week:

Day 1	Day 2	Day 3	Day 4	Day 5	Day 6
_____ min.	_____ min.	_____ min.	_____ min.	_____ min.	_____ min.

Problems I'm having or questions to ask at my next voice lesson:

Practice Log

	Day 4	Day 5	Day 6
Time of day			
Before practice I feel…			
Concept I'm working on			
Warm-ups	Yes / No	Yes / No	Yes / No
Technique exercises			
What went well or didn't go well with the technique exercises			
Song name			
What went well			
What needs work			
After practice I feel…			

Week: _____

This week's focus:

Notes from my voice lesson:

Practice Log

	Day 1	Day 2	Day 3
Time of day			
Before practice I feel...			
Concept I'm working on			
Warm-ups	Yes / No	Yes / No	Yes / No
Technique exercises			
What went well or didn't go well with the technique exercises			
Song name			
What went well			
What needs Work			
After practice I feel...			

Time invested this week:

Day 1	Day 2	Day 3	Day 4	Day 5	Day 6
_____ min.	_____ min.	_____ min.	_____ min.	_____ min.	_____ min.

Problems I'm having or questions to ask at my next voice lesson:

Practice Log

	Day 4	Day 5	Day 6
Time of day			
Before practice I feel...			
Concept I'm working on			
Warm-ups	Yes / No	Yes / No	Yes / No
Technique exercises			
What went well or didn't go well with the technique exercises			
Song name			
What went well			
What needs work			
After practice I feel...			

Week: _____

This week's focus:

Notes from my voice lesson:

Practice Log

	Day 1	Day 2	Day 3
Time of day			
Before practice I feel…			
Concept I'm working on			
Warm-ups	Yes / No	Yes / No	Yes / No
Technique exercises			
What went well or didn't go well with the technique exercises			
Song name			
What went well			
What needs Work			
After practice I feel…			

Time invested this week:

Day 1	Day 2	Day 3	Day 4	Day 5	Day 6
_____ min.	_____ min.	_____ min.	_____ min.	_____ min.	_____ min.

Problems I'm having or questions to ask at my next voice lesson:

Practice Log

	Day 4	Day 5	Day 6
Time of day			
Before practice I feel…			
Concept I'm working on			
Warm-ups	Yes / No	Yes / No	Yes / No
Technique exercises			
What went well or didn't go well with the technique exercises			
Song name			
What went well			
What needs work			
After practice I feel…			

Week: _____

This week's focus:

Notes from my voice lesson:

Practice Log

	Day 1	Day 2	Day 3
Time of day			
Before practice I feel...			
Concept I'm working on			
Warm-ups	Yes / No	Yes / No	Yes / No
Technique exercises			
What went well or didn't go well with the technique exercises			
Song name			
What went well			
What needs Work			
After practice I feel...			

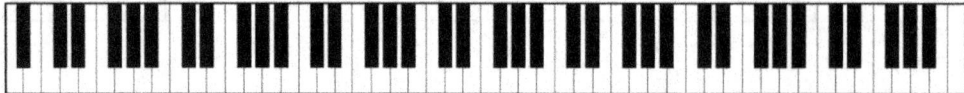

Time invested this week:

Day 1	Day 2	Day 3	Day 4	Day 5	Day 6
_____ min.	_____ min.	_____ min.	_____ min.	_____ min.	_____ min.

Problems I'm having or questions to ask at my next voice lesson:

Practice Log

	Day 4	Day 5	Day 6
Time of day			
Before practice I feel...			
Concept I'm working on			
Warm-ups	Yes / No	Yes / No	Yes / No
Technique exercises			
What went well or didn't go well with the technique exercises			
Song name			
What went well			
What needs work			
After practice I feel...			

Week: _____

This week's focus:

Notes from my voice lesson:

Practice Log

	Day 1	Day 2	Day 3
Time of day			
Before practice I feel...			
Concept I'm working on			
Warm-ups	Yes / No	Yes / No	Yes / No
Technique exercises			
What went well or didn't go well with the technique exercises			
Song name			
What went well			
What needs Work			
After practice I feel...			

Time invested this week:

Day 1	Day 2	Day 3	Day 4	Day 5	Day 6
_____ min.	_____ min.	_____ min.	_____ min.	_____ min.	_____ min.

Problems I'm having or questions to ask at my next voice lesson:

Practice Log

	Day 4	Day 5	Day 6
Time of day			
Before practice I feel…			
Concept I'm working on			
Warm-ups	Yes / No	Yes / No	Yes / No
Technique exercises			
What went well or didn't go well with the technique exercises			
Song name			
What went well			
What needs work			
After practice I feel…			

Week: _____

This week's focus:

Notes from my voice lesson:

Practice Log

	Day 1	Day 2	Day 3
Time of day			
Before practice I feel...			
Concept I'm working on			
Warm-ups	Yes / No	Yes / No	Yes / No
Technique exercises			
What went well or didn't go well with the technique exercises			
Song name			
What went well			
What needs Work			
After practice I feel...			

Time invested this week:

Day 1	Day 2	Day 3	Day 4	Day 5	Day 6
_____ min.	_____ min.	_____ min.	_____ min.	_____ min.	_____ min.

Problems I'm having or questions to ask at my next voice lesson:

Practice Log

	Day 4	Day 5	Day 6
Time of day			
Before practice I feel...			
Concept I'm working on			
Warm-ups	Yes / No	Yes / No	Yes / No
Technique exercises			
What went well or didn't go well with the technique exercises			
Song name			
What went well			
What needs work			
After practice I feel...			

Week: _____

This week's focus:

Notes from my voice lesson:

Practice Log

	Day 1	Day 2	Day 3
Time of day			
Before practice I feel...			
Concept I'm working on			
Warm-ups	Yes / No	Yes / No	Yes / No
Technique exercises			
What went well or didn't go well with the technique exercises			
Song name			
What went well			
What needs Work			
After practice I feel...			

Time invested this week:

Day 1	Day 2	Day 3	Day 4	Day 5	Day 6
_____ min.	_____ min.	_____ min.	_____ min.	_____ min.	_____ min.

Problems I'm having or questions to ask at my next voice lesson:

Practice Log

	Day 4	Day 5	Day 6
Time of day			
Before practice I feel...			
Concept I'm working on			
Warm-ups	Yes / No	Yes / No	Yes / No
Technique exercises			
What went well or didn't go well with the technique exercises			
Song name			
What went well			
What needs work			
After practice I feel...			

Week: _____

Notes from my voice lesson:

This week's focus:

Notes from my voice lesson:

Practice Log

	Day 1	Day 2	Day 3
Time of day			
Before practice I feel...			
Concept I'm working on			
Warm-ups	Yes / No	Yes / No	Yes / No
Technique exercises			
What went well or didn't go well with the technique exercises			
Song name			
What went well			
What needs Work			
After practice I feel...			

Time invested this week:

Day 1	Day 2	Day 3	Day 4	Day 5	Day 6
_____ min.	_____ min.	_____ min.	_____ min.	_____ min.	_____ min.

Problems I'm having or questions to ask at my next voice lesson:

Practice Log

	Day 4	Day 5	Day 6
Time of day			
Before practice I feel...			
Concept I'm working on			
Warm-ups	Yes / No	Yes / No	Yes / No
Technique exercises			
What went well or didn't go well with the technique exercises			
Song name			
What went well			
What needs work			
After practice I feel...			

Week: _____

This week's focus:

Notes from my voice lesson:

Practice Log

	Day 1	Day 2	Day 3
Time of day			
Before practice I feel…			
Concept I'm working on			
Warm-ups	Yes / No	Yes / No	Yes / No
Technique exercises			
What went well or didn't go well with the technique exercises			
Song name			
What went well			
What needs Work			
After practice I feel…			

Time invested this week:

Day 1	Day 2	Day 3	Day 4	Day 5	Day 6
_____ min.	_____ min.	_____ min.	_____ min.	_____ min.	_____ min.

Problems I'm having or questions to ask at my next voice lesson:

Practice Log

	Day 4	Day 5	Day 6
Time of day			
Before practice I feel...			
Concept I'm working on			
Warm-ups	Yes / No	Yes / No	Yes / No
Technique exercises			
What went well or didn't go well with the technique exercises			
Song name			
What went well			
What needs work			
After practice I feel...			

Week: _____

This week's focus:

Notes from my voice lesson:

Practice Log

	Day 1	Day 2	Day 3
Time of day			
Before practice I feel...			
Concept I'm working on			
Warm-ups	Yes / No	Yes / No	Yes / No
Technique exercises			
What went well or didn't go well with the technique exercises			
Song name			
What went well			
What needs Work			
After practice I feel...			

Time invested this week:

Day 1	Day 2	Day 3	Day 4	Day 5	Day 6
_____ min.	_____ min.	_____ min.	_____ min.	_____ min.	_____ min.

Problems I'm having or questions to ask at my next voice lesson:

Practice Log

	Day 4	Day 5	Day 6
Time of day			
Before practice I feel...			
Concept I'm working on			
Warm-ups	Yes / No	Yes / No	Yes / No
Technique exercises			
What went well or didn't go well with the technique exercises			
Song name			
What went well			
What needs work			
After practice I feel...			

Week: _____

This week's focus:

Notes from my voice lesson:

Practice Log

	Day 1	Day 2	Day 3
Time of day			
Before practice I feel…			
Concept I'm working on			
Warm-ups	Yes / No	Yes / No	Yes / No
Technique exercises			
What went well or didn't go well with the technique exercises			
Song name			
What went well			
What needs Work			
After practice I feel…			

Time invested this week:

Day 1	Day 2	Day 3	Day 4	Day 5	Day 6
_____ min.	_____ min.	_____ min.	_____ min.	_____ min.	_____ min.

Problems I'm having or questions to ask at my next voice lesson:

Practice Log

	Day 4	Day 5	Day 6
Time of day			
Before practice I feel...			
Concept I'm working on			
Warm-ups	Yes / No	Yes / No	Yes / No
Technique exercises			
What went well or didn't go well with the technique exercises			
Song name			
What went well			
What needs work			
After practice I feel...			

Week: _____

This week's focus:

Notes from my voice lesson:

Practice Log

	Day 1	Day 2	Day 3
Time of day			
Before practice I feel...			
Concept I'm working on			
Warm-ups	Yes / No	Yes / No	Yes / No
Technique exercises			
What went well or didn't go well with the technique exercises			
Song name			
What went well			
What needs Work			
After practice I feel...			

Time invested this week:

Day 1	Day 2	Day 3	Day 4	Day 5	Day 6
_____ min.	_____ min.	_____ min.	_____ min.	_____ min.	_____ min.

Problems I'm having or questions to ask at my next voice lesson:

Practice Log

	Day 4	Day 5	Day 6
Time of day			
Before practice I feel…			
Concept I'm working on			
Warm-ups	Yes / No	Yes / No	Yes / No
Technique exercises			
What went well or didn't go well with the technique exercises			
Song name			
What went well			
What needs work			
After practice I feel…			

Week: _____

This week's focus:

Notes from my voice lesson:

Practice Log

	Day 1	Day 2	Day 3
Time of day			
Before practice I feel…			
Concept I'm working on			
Warm-ups	Yes / No	Yes / No	Yes / No
Technique exercises			
What went well or didn't go well with the technique exercises			
Song name			
What went well			
What needs Work			
After practice I feel…			

Time invested this week:

Day 1	Day 2	Day 3	Day 4	Day 5	Day 6
_____ min.	_____ min.	_____ min.	_____ min.	_____ min.	_____ min.

Problems I'm having or questions to ask at my next voice lesson:

Practice Log

	Day 4	Day 5	Day 6
Time of day			
Before practice I feel...			
Concept I'm working on			
Warm-ups	Yes / No	Yes / No	Yes / No
Technique exercises			
What went well or didn't go well with the technique exercises			
Song name			
What went well			
What needs work			
After practice I feel...			

Week: _____

This week's focus:

Notes from my voice lesson:

Practice Log

	Day 1	Day 2	Day 3
Time of day			
Before practice I feel…			
Concept I'm working on			
Warm-ups	Yes / No	Yes / No	Yes / No
Technique exercises			
What went well or didn't go well with the technique exercises			
Song name			
What went well			
What needs Work			
After practice I feel…			

Time invested this week:

Day 1	Day 2	Day 3	Day 4	Day 5	Day 6
_____ min.	_____ min.	_____ min.	_____ min.	_____ min.	_____ min.

Problems I'm having or questions to ask at my next voice lesson:

Practice Log

	Day 4	Day 5	Day 6
Time of day			
Before practice I feel...			
Concept I'm working on			
Warm-ups	Yes / No	Yes / No	Yes / No
Technique exercises			
What went well or didn't go well with the technique exercises			
Song name			
What went well			
What needs work			
After practice I feel...			

Week: _____

This week's focus:

Notes from my voice lesson:

Practice Log

	Day 1	Day 2	Day 3
Time of day			
Before practice I feel…			
Concept I'm working on			
Warm-ups	Yes / No	Yes / No	Yes / No
Technique exercises			
What went well or didn't go well with the technique exercises			
Song name			
What went well			
What needs Work			
After practice I feel…			

Time invested this week:

Day 1	Day 2	Day 3	Day 4	Day 5	Day 6
_____ min.	_____ min.	_____ min.	_____ min.	_____ min.	_____ min.

Problems I'm having or questions to ask at my next voice lesson:

Practice Log

	Day 4	Day 5	Day 6
Time of day			
Before practice I feel…			
Concept I'm working on			
Warm-ups	Yes / No	Yes / No	Yes / No
Technique exercises			
What went well or didn't go well with the technique exercises			
Song name			
What went well			
What needs work			
After practice I feel…			

Week: _____

This week's focus:

Notes from my voice lesson:

Practice Log

	Day 1	Day 2	Day 3
Time of day			
Before practice I feel…			
Concept I'm working on			
Warm-ups	Yes / No	Yes / No	Yes / No
Technique exercises			
What went well or didn't go well with the technique exercises			
Song name			
What went well			
What needs Work			
After practice I feel…			

Time invested this week:

Day 1	Day 2	Day 3	Day 4	Day 5	Day 6
_____ min.	_____ min.	_____ min.	_____ min.	_____ min.	_____ min.

Problems I'm having or questions to ask at my next voice lesson:

Practice Log

	Day 4	Day 5	Day 6
Time of day			
Before practice I feel...			
Concept I'm working on			
Warm-ups	Yes / No	Yes / No	Yes / No
Technique exercises			
What went well or didn't go well with the technique exercises			
Song name			
What went well			
What needs work			
After practice I feel...			

Week: _____

This week's focus:

Notes from my voice lesson:

Practice Log

	Day 1	Day 2	Day 3
Time of day			
Before practice I feel…			
Concept I'm working on			
Warm-ups	Yes / No	Yes / No	Yes / No
Technique exercises			
What went well or didn't go well with the technique exercises			
Song name			
What went well			
What needs Work			
After practice I feel…			

Time invested this week:

Day 1	Day 2	Day 3	Day 4	Day 5	Day 6
_____ min.	_____ min.	_____ min.	_____ min.	_____ min.	_____ min.

Problems I'm having or questions to ask at my next voice lesson:

Practice Log

	Day 4	Day 5	Day 6
Time of day			
Before practice I feel...			
Concept I'm working on			
Warm-ups	Yes / No	Yes / No	Yes / No
Technique exercises			
What went well or didn't go well with the technique exercises			
Song name			
What went well			
What needs work			
After practice I feel...			

Week: _____

This week's focus:

Notes from my voice lesson:

Practice Log

	Day 1	Day 2	Day 3
Time of day			
Before practice I feel…			
Concept I'm working on			
Warm-ups	Yes / No	Yes / No	Yes / No
Technique exercises			
What went well or didn't go well with the technique exercises			
Song name			
What went well			
What needs Work			
After practice I feel…			

Time invested this week:

Day 1	Day 2	Day 3	Day 4	Day 5	Day 6
_____ min.	_____ min.	_____ min.	_____ min.	_____ min.	_____ min.

Problems I'm having or questions to ask at my next voice lesson:

Practice Log

	Day 4	Day 5	Day 6
Time of day			
Before practice I feel...			
Concept I'm working on			
Warm-ups	Yes / No	Yes / No	Yes / No
Technique exercises			
What went well or didn't go well with the technique exercises			
Song name			
What went well			
What needs work			
After practice I feel...			

Week: _____

This week's focus:

Notes from my voice lesson:

Practice Log

	Day 1	Day 2	Day 3
Time of day			
Before practice I feel...			
Concept I'm working on			
Warm-ups	Yes / No	Yes / No	Yes / No
Technique exercises			
What went well or didn't go well with the technique exercises			
Song name			
What went well			
What needs Work			
After practice I feel...			

Time invested this week:

Day 1	Day 2	Day 3	Day 4	Day 5	Day 6
_____ min.	_____ min.	_____ min.	_____ min.	_____ min.	_____ min.

Problems I'm having or questions to ask at my next voice lesson:

Practice Log

	Day 4	Day 5	Day 6
Time of day			
Before practice I feel...			
Concept I'm working on			
Warm-ups	Yes / No	Yes / No	Yes / No
Technique exercises			
What went well or didn't go well with the technique exercises			
Song name			
What went well			
What needs work			
After practice I feel...			

Week: _____

This week's focus:

Notes from my voice lesson:

Practice Log

	Day 1	Day 2	Day 3
Time of day			
Before practice I feel...			
Concept I'm working on			
Warm-ups	Yes / No	Yes / No	Yes / No
Technique exercises			
What went well or didn't go well with the technique exercises			
Song name			
What went well			
What needs Work			
After practice I feel...			

Time invested this week:

Day 1	Day 2	Day 3	Day 4	Day 5	Day 6
_____ min.	_____ min.	_____ min.	_____ min.	_____ min.	_____ min.

Problems I'm having or questions to ask at my next voice lesson:

Practice Log

	Day 4	Day 5	Day 6
Time of day			
Before practice I feel...			
Concept I'm working on			
Warm-ups	Yes / No	Yes / No	Yes / No
Technique exercises			
What went well or didn't go well with the technique exercises			
Song name			
What went well			
What needs work			
After practice I feel...			

Week: _____

This week's focus:

Notes from my voice lesson:

Practice Log

	Day 1	Day 2	Day 3
Time of day			
Before practice I feel...			
Concept I'm working on			
Warm-ups	Yes / No	Yes / No	Yes / No
Technique exercises			
What went well or didn't go well with the technique exercises			
Song name			
What went well			
What needs Work			
After practice I feel...			

Time invested this week:

Day 1	Day 2	Day 3	Day 4	Day 5	Day 6
_____ min.	_____ min.	_____ min.	_____ min.	_____ min.	_____ min.

Problems I'm having or questions to ask at my next voice lesson:

Practice Log

	Day 4	Day 5	Day 6
Time of day			
Before practice I feel…			
Concept I'm working on			
Warm-ups	Yes / No	Yes / No	Yes / No
Technique exercises			
What went well or didn't go well with the technique exercises			
Song name			
What went well			
What needs work			
After practice I feel…			

Week: _____

This week's focus:

Notes from my voice lesson:

Practice Log

	Day 1	Day 2	Day 3
Time of day			
Before practice I feel…			
Concept I'm working on			
Warm-ups	Yes / No	Yes / No	Yes / No
Technique exercises			
What went well or didn't go well with the technique exercises			
Song name			
What went well			
What needs Work			
After practice I feel…			

Time invested this week:

Day 1	Day 2	Day 3	Day 4	Day 5	Day 6
_____ min.	_____ min.	_____ min.	_____ min.	_____ min.	_____ min.

Problems I'm having or questions to ask at my next voice lesson:

Practice Log

	Day 4	Day 5	Day 6
Time of day			
Before practice I feel…			
Concept I'm working on			
Warm-ups	Yes / No	Yes / No	Yes / No
Technique exercises			
What went well or didn't go well with the technique exercises			
Song name			
What went well			
What needs work			
After practice I feel…			

Week: _____

This week's focus:

Notes from my voice lesson:

Practice Log

	Day 1	Day 2	Day 3
Time of day			
Before practice I feel…			
Concept I'm working on			
Warm-ups	Yes / No	Yes / No	Yes / No
Technique exercises			
What went well or didn't go well with the technique exercises			
Song name			
What went well			
What needs Work			
After practice I feel…			

Time invested this week:

Day 1	Day 2	Day 3	Day 4	Day 5	Day 6
_____ min.	_____ min.	_____ min.	_____ min.	_____ min.	_____ min.

Problems I'm having or questions to ask at my next voice lesson:

Practice Log

	Day 4	Day 5	Day 6
Time of day			
Before practice I feel...			
Concept I'm working on			
Warm-ups	Yes / No	Yes / No	Yes / No
Technique exercises			
What went well or didn't go well with the technique exercises			
Song name			
What went well			
What needs work			
After practice I feel...			

Week: _____

This week's focus:

Notes from my voice lesson:

Practice Log

	Day 1	Day 2	Day 3
Time of day			
Before practice I feel...			
Concept I'm working on			
Warm-ups	Yes / No	Yes / No	Yes / No
Technique exercises			
What went well or didn't go well with the technique exercises			
Song name			
What went well			
What needs Work			
After practice I feel...			

Time invested this week:

Day 1	Day 2	Day 3	Day 4	Day 5	Day 6
_____ min.	_____ min.	_____ min.	_____ min.	_____ min.	_____ min.

Problems I'm having or questions to ask at my next voice lesson:

Practice Log

	Day 4	Day 5	Day 6
Time of day			
Before practice I feel...			
Concept I'm working on			
Warm-ups	Yes / No	Yes / No	Yes / No
Technique exercises			
What went well or didn't go well with the technique exercises			
Song name			
What went well			
What needs work			
After practice I feel...			

Week: _____

This week's focus:

Notes from my voice lesson:

Practice Log

	Day 1	Day 2	Day 3
Time of day			
Before practice I feel...			
Concept I'm working on			
Warm-ups	Yes / No	Yes / No	Yes / No
Technique exercises			
What went well or didn't go well with the technique exercises			
Song name			
What went well			
What needs Work			
After practice I feel...			

Time invested this week:

Day 1	Day 2	Day 3	Day 4	Day 5	Day 6
_____ min.	_____ min.	_____ min.	_____ min.	_____ min.	_____ min.

Problems I'm having or questions to ask at my next voice lesson:

Practice Log

	Day 4	Day 5	Day 6
Time of day			
Before practice I feel...			
Concept I'm working on			
Warm-ups	Yes / No	Yes / No	Yes / No
Technique exercises			
What went well or didn't go well with the technique exercises			
Song name			
What went well			
What needs work			
After practice I feel...			

Week: _____

This week's focus:

Notes from my voice lesson:

Practice Log

	Day 1	Day 2	Day 3
Time of day			
Before practice I feel…			
Concept I'm working on			
Warm-ups	Yes / No	Yes / No	Yes / No
Technique exercises			
What went well or didn't go well with the technique exercises			
Song name			
What went well			
What needs Work			
After practice I feel…			

Time invested this week:

Day 1	Day 2	Day 3	Day 4	Day 5	Day 6
_____ min.	_____ min.	_____ min.	_____ min.	_____ min.	_____ min.

Problems I'm having or questions to ask at my next voice lesson:

Practice Log

	Day 4	Day 5	Day 6
Time of day			
Before practice I feel...			
Concept I'm working on			
Warm-ups	Yes / No	Yes / No	Yes / No
Technique exercises			
What went well or didn't go well with the technique exercises			
Song name			
What went well			
What needs work			
After practice I feel...			

Week: _____

This week's focus:

Notes from my voice lesson:

Practice Log

	Day 1	Day 2	Day 3
Time of day			
Before practice I feel…			
Concept I'm working on			
Warm-ups	Yes / No	Yes / No	Yes / No
Technique exercises			
What went well or didn't go well with the technique exercises			
Song name			
What went well			
What needs Work			
After practice I feel…			

Time invested this week:

Day 1	Day 2	Day 3	Day 4	Day 5	Day 6
_____ min.	_____ min.	_____ min.	_____ min.	_____ min.	_____ min.

Problems I'm having or questions to ask at my next voice lesson:

Practice Log

	Day 4	Day 5	Day 6
Time of day			
Before practice I feel…			
Concept I'm working on			
Warm-ups	Yes / No	Yes / No	Yes / No
Technique exercises			
What went well or didn't go well with the technique exercises			
Song name			
What went well			
What needs work			
After practice I feel…			

Week: _____

This week's focus:

Notes from my voice lesson:

Practice Log

	Day 1	Day 2	Day 3
Time of day			
Before practice I feel…			
Concept I'm working on			
Warm-ups	Yes / No	Yes / No	Yes / No
Technique exercises			
What went well or didn't go well with the technique exercises			
Song name			
What went well			
What needs Work			
After practice I feel…			

Time invested this week:

Day 1	Day 2	Day 3	Day 4	Day 5	Day 6
_____ min.	_____ min.	_____ min.	_____ min.	_____ min.	_____ min.

Problems I'm having or questions to ask at my next voice lesson:

Practice Log

	Day 4	Day 5	Day 6
Time of day			
Before practice I feel...			
Concept I'm working on			
Warm-ups	Yes / No	Yes / No	Yes / No
Technique exercises			
What went well or didn't go well with the technique exercises			
Song name			
What went well			
What needs work			
After practice I feel...			

Week: _____

This week's focus:

Notes from my voice lesson:

Practice Log

	Day 1	Day 2	Day 3
Time of day			
Before practice I feel...			
Concept I'm working on			
Warm-ups	Yes / No	Yes / No	Yes / No
Technique exercises			
What went well or didn't go well with the technique exercises			
Song name			
What went well			
What needs Work			
After practice I feel...			

Time invested this week:

Day 1	Day 2	Day 3	Day 4	Day 5	Day 6
_____ min.	_____ min.	_____ min.	_____ min.	_____ min.	_____ min.

Problems I'm having or questions to ask at my next voice lesson:

Practice Log

	Day 4	Day 5	Day 6
Time of day			
Before practice I feel…			
Concept I'm working on			
Warm-ups	Yes / No	Yes / No	Yes / No
Technique exercises			
What went well or didn't go well with the technique exercises			
Song name			
What went well			
What needs work			
After practice I feel…			

Week: _____

This week's focus:

Notes from my voice lesson:

Practice Log

	Day 1	Day 2	Day 3
Time of day			
Before practice I feel…			
Concept I'm working on			
Warm-ups	Yes / No	Yes / No	Yes / No
Technique exercises			
What went well or didn't go well with the technique exercises			
Song name			
What went well			
What needs Work			
After practice I feel…			

Time invested this week:

Day 1	Day 2	Day 3	Day 4	Day 5	Day 6
_____ min.	_____ min.	_____ min.	_____ min.	_____ min.	_____ min.

Problems I'm having or questions to ask at my next voice lesson:

Practice Log

	Day 4	Day 5	Day 6
Time of day			
Before practice I feel...			
Concept I'm working on			
Warm-ups	Yes / No	Yes / No	Yes / No
Technique exercises			
What went well or didn't go well with the technique exercises			
Song name			
What went well			
What needs work			
After practice I feel...			

Week: _____

This week's focus:

Notes from my voice lesson:

Practice Log

	Day 1	Day 2	Day 3
Time of day			
Before practice I feel…			
Concept I'm working on			
Warm-ups	Yes / No	Yes / No	Yes / No
Technique exercises			
What went well or didn't go well with the technique exercises			
Song name			
What went well			
What needs Work			
After practice I feel…			

Time invested this week:

Day 1	Day 2	Day 3	Day 4	Day 5	Day 6
_____ min.	_____ min.	_____ min.	_____ min.	_____ min.	_____ min.

Problems I'm having or questions to ask at my next voice lesson:

Practice Log

	Day 4	Day 5	Day 6
Time of day			
Before practice I feel...			
Concept I'm working on			
Warm-ups	Yes / No	Yes / No	Yes / No
Technique exercises			
What went well or didn't go well with the technique exercises			
Song name			
What went well			
What needs work			
After practice I feel...			

Week: _____

This week's focus:

Notes from my voice lesson:

Practice Log

	Day 1	Day 2	Day 3
Time of day			
Before practice I feel…			
Concept I'm working on			
Warm-ups	Yes / No	Yes / No	Yes / No
Technique exercises			
What went well or didn't go well with the technique exercises			
Song name			
What went well			
What needs Work			
After practice I feel…			

Time invested this week:

Day 1	Day 2	Day 3	Day 4	Day 5	Day 6
_____ min.	_____ min.	_____ min.	_____ min.	_____ min.	_____ min.

Problems I'm having or questions to ask at my next voice lesson:

Practice Log

	Day 4	Day 5	Day 6
Time of day			
Before practice I feel…			
Concept I'm working on			
Warm-ups	Yes / No	Yes / No	Yes / No
Technique exercises			
What went well or didn't go well with the technique exercises			
Song name			
What went well			
What needs work			
After practice I feel…			

Notes:

Appendix

Consonants

Compression	Decompression
B D G	*CH *F *H *K *P *T *TH J Z M N NG
	*Cords aren't doing anything

BREATH SUPPORT
All Fricatives give breath support

VOICED FRICATIVES	UNVOICED FRICATIVES
J V Z ZH Voiced TH	CH F S SH Unvoiced TH Can't sing on an unvoiced fricative

EMBOUCHURE	NASALS
NARROW	DROPS SOFT PALATE
B F P *W	M N NG
*Most extreme embouchure closure	Decompression

TONGUE POSITION

LETTER	WHAT IT DOES
CH	Brings tongue forward
G	Tall tongue in the back *fixes problems if singer wants to pull tongue down or back
J	Frontal in the mouth
K	Tall tongue in the back
*W	*Approximants: Doesn't block completely, needs nasal. ("W" approx. the lips)
*Y	Tongue tall, back and free ("Y" approximates the tongue)
*L	Don't use L, R in exercises unless you want to fix it
*R	Tongue pulling back

Consonant Blends for Vocal Exercise Design

Features	Blend	Features
- voiced plosive - compression - narrow embouchure	BW	- lip narrowing - deals with lip spreading
- voiced plosive - compression - narrow embouchure	BL	- approximant - loosens lips, jaw & tongues - "Blah"
- voiced plosive - compression - narrow embouchure	BY	- approximant (needs nasal) - tongue tall at back
- unvoiced fricative - decompression - breath support	FW	- small embouchure - approximant (needs nasal)
- unvoiced fricative - decompression - breath support	FY	- approximant (needs nasal) - tongue tall at back
- strength - compression	GW	- small embouchure - approximant (needs nasal)
- strength - compression	GY	- approximant (needs nasal) - tongue tall at back
- unvoiced fricative - unvoiced plosive - tongue tall in back - decompression	KW	- small embouchure - approximant (needs nasal)
- unvoiced fricative - unvoiced plosive - tongue tall in back - decompression	KY	- approximant (needs nasal) - tongue tall at back
- approximant (needs nasal)	LW	- small embouchure - approximant (needs nasal)
- nasal - lowered soft palate - decompression - CT dominant	MW	- small embouchure - approximant (needs nasal)
- nasal - lowered soft palate - decompression - CT dominant	MY	- approximant (needs nasal) - tongue tall at back
- nasal - lowered soft palate - decompression - CT dominant	NW	- small embouchure - approximant (needs nasal)
- nasal - lowered soft palate - decompression - CT dominant	NY	- approximant (needs nasal) - tongue tall at back
- unvoiced fricative - breath support - decompression	SK	- unvoiced plosive - unvoiced fricative - decompression - tongue tall in back
- unvoiced fricative - breath support - decompression	SM	- nasal - lowered soft palate - decompression - CT dominant
- unvoiced fricative - breath support - decompression	SN	- nasal - lowered soft palate - decompression - CT dominant
- unvoiced fricative - breath support - decompression	SW	- small embouchure - approximant (needs nasal)
- voiced fricative - breath support - decompression	VW	- small embouchure - approximant (needs nasal)
- voiced fricative - breath support - decompression	VY	- approximant (needs nasal) - tongue tall at back
- voiced fricative - breath support - decompression	ZW	- small embouchure - approximant (needs nasal)
- voiced fricative - breath support - decompression	ZM	- nasal - lowered soft palate - decompression - CT dominant
- voiced fricative - breath support - decompression	ZN	- nasal - lowered soft palate - decompression - CT dominant - eg. "zznaaa"

Monophthongs
(one vowel)

Vowel		Benefits	Limitations
/iy/	beet	- brightest - headiest (tongue is blocking mouth) - brings tongue up & forward - helps with twang	- higher larynx at times - weak - extreme vowel - tends toward tension
/i/	bit	- bright & heady (tongue blocking mouth) - tongue in front - helps with twang - not as extreme as /iy/ beet	
/ae/	bat	- more mouth dominant (belty) - chestier - still bright & twangy	
/e/	bet	- neutral vowel - not extreme - you can hear the singer better - good if the singer needs to hear themselves	

/a/	hot (ah)	- chestiest vowel (mouth exit is biggest=good for belting)
		- brings up strength
		- most open mouth
		- lowest tongue
		- least head resistance
		- low larynx
			- tend to push it out because there's no resistance
			    tongue down
			    mouth open
			- hard to get head resonance

/uh/	but	- neutral dark vowel	
/ow/	bought	- chesty dark vowel - lip rounding vowel - use when singer spreads too much - keeps lip embouchure - strong & dark	- can be harder to belt with darker vowels
/oo/	boot	- headiest of all vowels - darkness - helps when singer spreads too much - helps with larynx lowering - flexible, good for light singing	- can be harder to belt with darker vowels
/u/	foot	- heady & flexible - best for larynx lowering - dark & deep	- can be harder to belt with darker vowels

Dipthongs
(two vowel)

Compound exercise-- two exercises for the price of one

Dipthong	1st Vowel	Benefits	2nd Vowel	Benefit
ie (my)	I	Strong, chestier	E	Flexible, bright, heady
oh (go)	O	Dark, gives depth	O (w)	Flexible, heady
ao (ow)	A	Strongest vowel	O	Flexible
oe (oy)	O	Dark	E	Bright
ay (ae)	A	Bright, chesty, strong	E	Bright, heady, flexible

Author Bio

Juanita grew up in Southwestern Ontario and has stubbornly refused to move from that area as she confidently believes it is the most beautiful place on earth to live… except during the winter months. She lives with her husband, two sons and two goldfish who are currently grieving the loss of the third goldfish as it explored the filter and did not find the inside of the filter to be conducive to living.

Juanita and her family live in the beautiful town of Ingersoll where she runs J.R. Vocal Coaching out of her home studio.

Passionate about music
Juanita has always loved music—instrumental and vocal.
However, like many people, she used to believe that she was stuck with the voice she was born with. It wasn't until she had the opportunity to take lessons from a very gifted vocal coach that she realized that through warm-ups and technique exercises, she could strengthen her voice, expand her range, and ultimately sing the way she never dreamed she could!

Passionate about teaching
Juanita eventually realized that as much as she loved singing, she was born to teach. Juanita is energized by teaching and showing students that their vocal roadblocks are actually only hurdles.

Trained by the best
Juanita was trained and mentored by Justin Stoney, owner and founder of New York Vocal Coaching. Through and through, Justin is an inspiring and gifted teacher as well as someone who has worked tirelessly to perfect his craft of singing and teaching. Juanita considers herself truly blessed to have been able to learn under him. Justin Stoney has encouraged her and given her the tools she needs to be the best teacher she can be.

I hope you found this journal helpful. I am always looking to improve the journal, and I am excited about hearing from you to learn not only how this book has helped you, but also to find out how I can make the book fit your needs more effectively. I can be contacted through my website at jrvocals.com or by email at jrvocalcoaching@gmail.com

If you enjoyed the book, please also take the time to leave a quick review where you purchased the book or on Amazon or Goodreads. Reviews can help other students know if this book will be beneficial to them.

All the best to you as you continue to perfect your singing voice!

Books by Juanita Robinson
J.R. Vocal Coaching

Practice Planner

The J.R. Vocal Coaching Practice Planner is a simple planner to assist vocalists and voice teachers to communicate expectations in an organized and effective manner.
This planner allows for the teacher to clearly lay out each vocal exercise, including an option to map out scales on an image of a piano keyboard. All you, the student, have to do is to work through the assigned exercises each week. It's like having your teacher beside you each time you practice!

Practice Journal

The J.R. Vocal Coaching Practice Journal is an advanced journal which lays out all your vocal tools, keeping them organized and in one place. This daily vocal practice log is your chance to look for patterns that lead to success or find out what might be hindering your growth as a vocalist. This practical journal is exactly what you need to help you as you become the vocalist you've always wanted to be!

The Practice Planner for Vocalists & Voice Teachers and the Practice Journal for Vocalists can both be found on Amazon and most other online bookstores.

www.ingramcontent.com/pod-product-compliance
Lightning Source LLC
Chambersburg PA
CBHW081154070526
44583CB00021B/2835